Spring Harvest Bible Workbook

ESTHER

A Woman of Influence

Elizabeth McQuoid

Series editor for Bible character workbooks – Ian Coffey

LIFESTYLE

SPRING HARVEST
Equipping the Church for action

CONTENTS

Leaders' Guide

ABOUT THIS BOOK

This book is written primarily for a group situation, but can easily be used by individuals who want to study the book of Esther. It can be used in a variety of contexts, so it is perhaps helpful to spell out the assumptions that we have made about the groups that will use it. These can have a variety of names – homegroups, Bible study groups, cell groups – we've used housegroup as the generic term.

▶ The emphasis of the studies will be on the application of the Bible. Group members will not just learn facts, but will be encouraged to think 'How does this apply to me? What change does it require of me? What incidents or situations in my life is this relevant to?'

▶ Housegroups can encourage honesty and make space for questions and doubts. The aim of the studies is not to find the 'right answer', but to help members understand the Bible by working through their questions. The Christian faith throws up paradoxes. Events in people's lives may make particular verses difficult to understand. The housegroup should be a safe place to express these concerns.

▶ Housegroups can give opportunities for deep friendships to develop. Group members will be encouraged to talk about their experiences, feelings, questions, hopes and fears. They will be able to offer one another pastoral support and to get involved in each other's lives.

▶ There is a difference between being a collection of individuals who happen to meet together every Wednesday and being an effective group who bounce ideas off each other, spark inspiration and creativity, pooling their talents and resources to create solutions together: one whose whole is definitely greater than the sum of its parts. The process of working through these studies will encourage healthy group dynamics.

Space is given for you to write answers, comments, questions and thoughts. This book will not tell you what to think, but will help you discover the truth of God's word through thinking, discussing, praying and listening.

FOR GROUP MEMBERS

▶ You will probably get more out of the study if you spend some time during the week reading the passage and thinking about the questions. Make a note of anything you don't understand.

▶ Pray that God will help you to understand the passage and show you how to apply it. Pray for other members in the group, too, that they will find the study helpful.

▶ Be willing to take part in the discussions. The leader of the group is not there as an expert with all the answers. They will want everyone to get involved and share their thoughts and opinions.

▶ However, don't dominate the group! If you are aware that you are saying a lot, make space for others to contribute. Be sensitive to other group members and aim to be encouraging. If you disagree with someone, say so but without putting down their contribution.

FOR INDIVIDUALS

▶ Although this book is written with a group in mind, it can also be easily used by individuals. You obviously won't be able to do the group activities suggested, but you can consider how you would answer the questions and write your thoughts in the space provided.

▶ You may find it helpful to talk to a prayer partner about what you have learnt, and ask them to pray for you as you try and apply what you are learning to your life.

▶ The New International Version of the text is printed in the book. If you use a different version, then read from your own Bible as well.

Other titles in this Spring Harvest Bible Studies series:

BIBLE BOOKS

Exodus – Mission of God – ISBN 1-85078-496-5

Studies in Exodus based on the Spring Harvest 2003 theme, Shepherd's Bush to King's Cross.

Letters to the Churches – ISBN 1-85078-441-8

Studies in Revelation based on the Spring Harvest 2002 theme, You've Got Mail.

Sermon on the Mount – ISBN 1-85078-407-8

Studies in Matthew's gospel based on the Spring Harvest 2001 theme, King of the Hill.

Jesus at the Centre – ISBN 1-85078-440-X

Studies in John's gospel based on the Spring Harvest 2000 theme, A Royal Banquet.

Big Themes from Colossians – ISBN 1-85078-457-4

Studies in Colossians based on the Spring Harvest 1999 theme, Across the Borderline.

BIBLE CHARACTERS

David – After God's Own Heart – ISBN 1-85078-497-3

Based on selected chapters from Ian Coffey's book, *The Story of David*, ISBN 1-85078-485-X.

Jonah – God's Compassion – ISBN 1-85078-508-2

Studies on Jonah.

Moses – Friend of God – ISBN 1-85078-519-8

Studies on Moses.

Ruth – Love, Honour and Obey – ISBN 1-85078-536-8

Studies on Ruth.

BIBLE THEMES

Mission – Going Global – ISBN 1-85078-521-X

Based on Tim Jeffery and Steve Chalke's ground-breaking book *Connect!*, which rethinks mission for the 21st century.

INTRODUCTION

Dreams do come true – at least that's what the Jews and Esther in particular must have thought.

For the first time in a long time the Jews were enjoying the good life. Their initial fears and frustrations on being taken into exile in Babylon had subsided and, although Cyrus had allowed them to return to their homeland in 539BC, most of them had decided to stay in Babylon. Businesses were flourishing, people were making money, life was stable and secure – the Jews felt settled in this foreign land.

Esther, too, must have thought she was living in a dream world. Every little girl dreams of being a princess and here she was, the king of Persia's favourite wife, not just a princess but a queen. She lived in the palace of a man whose empire stretched, according to modern boundaries, from Pakistan to northern Sudan. She indulged in the finest food and most exquisite beauty treatments – opulent and extravagant were the only words to describe her new life.

Then, quite unexpectedly, disaster struck. The dream world of beauty pageants and palaces was turned on its head as the king issued an edict to exterminate the Jews. Court intrigue and deception had let evil loose and once again the Jewish nation was teetering on the brink of extinction. Their charmed existence had turned into the sickeningly familiar pattern of persecution at the hands of a ruthless enemy.

Overnight, Esther's privileged position brought with it a weighty responsibility as she represented her nation before the king. She showed herself to be more than a beauty icon or mannequin's model – in fact, she turned out to be a woman of faith and courage. Her initiative saved the Jewish people and today they still celebrate this deliverance with the festival of Purim.

For us the book of Esther is more than just a heroic tale of faith in action. It helps us see our own deliverance against the grand backdrop of salvation history; it reminds us that God, though hidden, is always at work; and it invites us to join the ordinary men and women of Bible times who represented God's will and purpose to the world. The world is as needy and secular as it was in Esther's day and God is still looking for those who will represent him. And who knows but that God planted you where you are 'for such a time as this'?

AN UNPROMISING SITUATION

Aim: To remember that God is at work in the most secular situation

Xerxes' palace, with all its excesses and debauchery, isn't the type of place where we'd like to take God. And yet this was just the setting in which he was going to be at work. Often we try to protect God – we think our work situation is too secular for him, our personal life too messy for him. And so we limit God to the religious activities and places where we think he'd feel comfortable and we forget that when he was on earth, some of his closest friends were tax collectors, prostitutes and sinners.

This is what happened during the time of Xerxes, the Xerxes who ruled over 127 provinces stretching from India to Cush: At that time King Xerxes reigned from his royal throne in the citadel of Susa, and in the third year of his reign he gave a banquet for all his nobles and officials. The military leaders of Persia and Media, the princes, and the nobles of the provinces were present.

For a full 180 days he displayed the vast wealth of his kingdom and the splendour and glory of his majesty. When these days were over, the king gave a banquet, lasting seven days, in the enclosed garden of the king's palace, for all the people from the least to the greatest, who were in the citadel of Susa. The garden had hangings of white and blue linen, fastened with cords of white linen and purple material to silver rings on marble pillars. There were couches of gold and silver on a mosaic pavement of porphyry, marble, mother-of-pearl and other costly stones. Wine was served in goblets of gold, each one different from the other, and the royal wine was abundant in keeping with the king's liberality. By the king's command each guest was allowed to drink in his own way, for the king instructed all the wine stewards to serve each man what he wished.

Esther 1:1–8

TO SET THE SCENE

WWJD – What Would Jesus Do? What do you think Jesus would have done if he'd been one of the nobles or military leaders invited to Xerxes' banquet?

What would you do?

▶ Decline the invitation knowing it would turn into an unsavoury event?

▶ Go to the banquet but only drink orange juice hoping that people would admire your Christian convictions?

▶ Go to the banquet, have a few drinks, try to mix with the other nobles and show that Christians can have a good time?

▶ Go to the banquet and get drunk like everyone else?

▶ Something else?

READ ESTHER 1:1-22

1 Think about the palace and court life that Esther would share.

2 Look for evidence from the text that Xerxes was:

▶ Rich

▶ Generous

▶ Used to getting his own way

▶ Easily influenced

3 What desires do you think influenced Xerxes' behaviour?

4 What would be your concerns for Esther given:

▶ The king's and nobles' treatment of Queen Vashti?

▶ The view of women held by those in the palace?

5 In the rest of the book we find that God used the secular excesses, the feasting and even king Xerxes to accomplish his plan. How does this reality expand your view of God?

6   Why do we separate God from the rest of our secular life?

HOW DOES THIS ... APPLY TO ME

7   How can we be more intentional about incorporating God into our:

▶ Work life?
▶ Family life?
▶ Social life?

ENGAGING WITH ... THE WORLD

8   Work is often the hardest place to share the gospel. In what ways can we bring a gospel perspective or God's point of view into the workplace?

HOW DOES THIS ... APPLY TO ME

9   We are God's hands and feet in the world, so if he is going to work in secular situations we need to be there too. What safeguards can we put in place to protect ourselves, our testimony and our faith in these situations?

WORSHIP

We may not like to bridge the culture gap from the sanctified to the secular but thank God that Jesus did! Thank God that Jesus left the delights of heaven to come to earth. Spend time meditating on the cost of God's salvation plan – look at Philippians 2:5–11, 2 Corinthians 8:9. Then pray together in twos that you might represent Christ well in the secular situations you'll be going into this week.

FOR FURTHER STUDY

Many of us find it difficult to share the gospel. Jim Petersen's *Living Proof* explains how we can do this naturally in an increasingly secular culture.

FOR NEXT WEEK

Look again at your answer to question 7. Take one practical step to incorporate God more fully into your work, family or social life. Get someone to ask you next week how you got on!

LIVING IN ENEMY TERRITORY

Aim: To re-examine how we live as Christians in the modern world

'Be in the world but not of it' is a much abused phrase! We've used it to legitimise the Christian club mentality and renege on one of our key roles – to reach with the gospel the 97% who don't come to church. But while we attempt to redress the balance we do need boundary markers – not to exclude others but to preserve the integrity of our faith and the purity of its message. In an ever-changing society, the ongoing debate is where these boundary lines should fall.

> *Now there was in the citadel of Susa a Jew of the tribe of Benjamin, named Mordecai son of Jair, the son of Shimei, the son of Kish, who had been carried into exile from Jerusalem by Nebuchadnezzar king of Babylon, among those taken captive with Jehoiachin king of Judah. Mordecai had a cousin named Hadasseh, whom he had brought up because she had neither father nor mother. This girl, who was also known as Esther, was lovely in form and features, and Mordecai had taken her as his own daughter when her father and mother had died.*
>
> *When the king's order and edict had been proclaimed, many girls were brought to the citadel of Susa and put under the care of Hegai. Esther was also taken to the king's palace and entrusted to Hegai, who had charge of the harem.*
>
> *Now the king was attracted to Esther more than to any of the other women, and she won his favour and approval more than any of the other virgins. So he set a royal crown on her head and made her queen instead of Vashti.*
>
> ***Esther 2:5–8, 17***

TO SET THE SCENE

Discuss how the boundary lines have changed in your own Christian experience. What were the Christian taboos twenty years ago, five years ago, and what are they today? What were/are the reasons behind these taboos? Do you think they're legitimate?

READ ESTHER 2:1-18

1   What further insights does this chapter give you into Xerxes' character and lifestyle?

2   In 2:5 we are introduced to Mordecai whose family had been taken into captivity (see also 2 Kgs. 24:8-14). Look at the following references to Mordecai's ancestors. Which king was he related to? This will become significant later in the story.

▶   1 Samuel 9:1-2
▶   2 Samuel 16:5

3   Esther probably had little choice about going into the harem but what is the evidence that she willingly complied once she got there?

4   Esther and Daniel were both exiles but they drew the boundary lines in different places (look at Dan. 1:1-8). How did they react differently to Jewish taboos?

5   Esther seemed to give up on the distinctives of her faith when she concealed her Jewish identity (2:10, 20).

▶   Why do you think she did this?
▶   How can we square this with Jesus' command to be salt and light in our communities (Mt. 5:13-16)?

6   Under what circumstances can you imagine it might be wise to keep quiet or at least to downplay your Christian commitment?

ENGAGING WITH

THE WORLD

7   Esther and later Mordecai (9:4, 10: 1–3) found that they could live and work well in enemy territory. What can we learn from their example about how we should interact with secular society?

HOW DOES THIS

?

APPLY TO ME

8   As with Esther and Daniel, all of us will draw the boundary markers in different places when it comes to our interaction with the secular world. Although there are no hard and fast rules, what do you think should be our guiding principles? (Look at Acts 5:29, Rom. 13: 1–7, 1 Pet. 2:13–17).

9   Some of us will be more vocal than others about our faith in our work or family situations. Describe an occasion where you have felt you had to take a stand as a Christian. What was the outcome?

WORSHIP

In silence, repent for the times you've failed to stand up for Christ when you should have done. As a group, confess the occasions when as a church you've been a closed community – the times when you've failed to address moral, social and even political issues as you ought. Light a candle as you meditate on what it means for you to be the light of the world in your own situation. If you feel able, you might like to pray in twos that God would give you wisdom to know where to draw the boundary lines in your family, work and social life.

FURTHER STUDY

John Stott's *Issues Facing Christians Today* gives helpful insights into the moral and social dilemmas that confront believers in the twenty-first century and upon which they may be required to take a stand.

A Long Way East Of Eden by Peter Lowman describes the postmodern secular world and how it points to our need to rediscover God.

ACTIVITY PAGE

We don't like to think that we're 'living in enemy territory' but we are. Every day we relate to people, businesses, a government and media that operate along secular lines. They have values and priorities that are totally at odds with our Christian worldview. So how do we relate? How can we be salt and light in these situations?

Consider the following scenarios. What would you do?

▶ You're starting a new job as an accountant. Will you announce that you're a Christian straight away to make your stand clear, will you hope your faith is obvious by the way you live and by making a few comments about church, or will you keep quiet about your convictions until you're asked to do some creative accounting?

▶ You're talking about witnessing with a friend who's just become a Christian. She says to you 'Sharing your faith all depends on your personality. If God made you quiet and shy, he's not going to expect you to speak about him to lots of other people.' Is she right?

▶ You're a church leader and two members of your congregation come to you for advice. One has been in a job for two years and is now being pressurised into working Sunday shifts. Another has a child in primary school where they have just announced they will not be celebrating Christmas for fear of offending those of other religions. Are these examples of occasions where Christians should take a stand or are they simply part of 'living in enemy territory'?

PERSONAL CONFLICTS

Aim: To remember the dangers of holding on to hatred and bitterness

Have you ever watched the news and asked yourself 'How did it come to this?' We see pictures on the television of war and combat and wonder how this latest dispute escalated so quickly. But we shouldn't really be surprised because we know from personal experience that hatred and bitterness have a habit of getting out of control. We may try to hide our feelings or excuse them, but sooner or later they can spread like wildfire and make us enemies – of others and of God.

> After these events, King Xerxes honoured Haman son of Hammedatha, the Agagite, elevating him and giving him a seat of honour higher than that of all the other nobles. All the royal officials at the king's gate knelt down and paid honour to Haman, for the king had commanded this concerning him. But Mordecai would not kneel down or pay him honour.
>
> Then the royal officials at the king's gate asked Mordecai, 'Why do you disobey the king's command?' Day after day they spoke to him but he refused to comply. Therefore they told Haman about it to see whether Mordecai's behaviour would be tolerated, for he had told them he was a Jew.
>
> When Haman saw that Mordecai would not kneel down or pay him honour, he was enraged. Yet having learned who Mordecai's people were, he scorned the idea of killing only Mordecai. Instead Haman looked for a way to destroy all Mordecai's people, the Jews, throughout the whole kingdom of Xerxes.
>
> **Esther 3:1–6**

TO SET THE SCENE

What image comes to mind when you think of the word 'enemy'? Who are our modern-day 'enemies' and are they easy to spot?

READ ESTHER 2:19–3:15

1   These verses begin to set up the contrast between Mordecai and Haman. How does the author do this in 2:21–3:2 in particular?

WHAT DOES **2**   The conflict between the two men is **SEARCH** presented as a historical one. Haman is described as an Agagite; Agag was king of **THE BIBLE SAY?** the Amalekites; Mordecai was an Israelite related to King Saul. Look at the following references to explain the enmity between the Amalekites and the Israelites:

> Exodus 17:8–16
> Deuteronomy 25:17–19
> 1 Samuel 15:1–8, 32–33

3   How did Haman make his personal grievance sound legitimate to the king?

4   Scan through 3:12–14. How does the author stress that all the Jews heard about and were affected by Haman's command?

5   Look at 3:7,12. How long was it between the announcement and the planned ethnic cleansing? How would this time delay work both for and against the Jews?

6   What do these verses tell us about the nature of personal hatred?

APPLY THIS TO **7**   Haman's hatred was rooted in racial prejudice. Do you recognise racism in your church/housegroup/heart?

MY CHURCH

HOW DOES THIS
APPLY TO ME

8   What are the practical ways we can deal with bitterness and prejudice, including racism, to stop it spreading and hurting us and other people?

9   The Amalekites were called God's enemies. Who do you think are God's enemies today? Do you ever find yourself in this category?

HOW DOES THIS
APPLY TO ME

10 What steps can we take to become friends rather than enemies of God?

WORSHIP

▶ In silence, confess areas of your life where you're behaving like an enemy of God (Jas. 4:4).

▶ Repent of any hatred you've been harbouring.

▶ Ask God's forgiveness for any racial prejudice you've felt and ask him to make you more sensitive to others.

▶ Spend some time as a group praising God for the possibility of being his friend, for the privilege of knowing him intimately (Jas. 2:23, Ex. 33:11).

▶ Pray for each other that you'd have the strength and faith to live like a friend of God rather than an enemy. If possible share and pray together about specific areas where you need to be obedient to God (Jn. 15:14).

FOR NEXT WEEK

Is there someone you need to apologise to, someone you need to forgive? However difficult this may be, take steps to address the problem this week and stop your bitterness spreading.

WHO IS IN CONTROL?

 Aim: To explore our role in God's plan

Teenagers in the party scene spend their cash trying to get out of control whilst most adults spend their energy trying to stay in control! As Christians, we say that God is in control but often we don't live as though this is true. We acknowledge his control as long as he does what we want, as long as our positions in church and work are secure, and as long as our families are doing well. But trusting that God is in control in the difficult times and finding out what part we should play whilst respecting that control are two of main issues Christians struggle with.

> *When Esther's words were reported to Mordecai, he sent back this answer: 'Do not think that because you are in the king's house you alone of all the Jews will escape. For if you remain silent at this time, relief and deliverance for the Jews will arise from another place, but you and your father's family will perish. And who knows but that you have come to royal position for such a time as this?'*
>
> *Then Esther sent this reply to Mordecai: 'Go, gather together all the Jews who are in Susa, and fast for me. Do not eat or drink for three days, night or day. I and my maids will fast as you do. When this is done, I will go to the king, even though it is against the law. And if I perish, I perish.'*
>
> *So Mordecai went away and carried out all of Esther's instructions.*
> **Esther 4:12–17**

TO SET THE SCENE

▶ On a scale of 1–10 (1 being 'slightly' and 10 being 'very much so') how would you rate yourself as a 'control freak'? To what extent do need to feel in control of people and situations?

▶ Under what circumstances have you found it most difficult to give up control?
  • When your child went off to university
  • When you had to hand over an unfinished project to a colleague at work
  • When you had to stand down from a church ministry

▶ What description best fits how you view God's control over your life?
- He is in complete control, pulling your strings like a puppet
- He is like an angry boss, setting impossibly high standards and waiting to reprimand your slightest failings
- He is like an understudy in a play, ready to take control when you need him
- He's like a film director, having the big picture in mind but wanting your views as to how to develop the detail of the plot
- Other

READ ESTHER 4:1–17

1 This is a crisis point in the story. What would be the consequences if Haman's orders were carried out? How would the story line of the Bible be affected?

2 Given how serious the situation was, why do you think Esther was reluctant to go and see the king? What do you think changed her mind?

3 From the two speeches in 4:13–16, what do you learn about the characters and beliefs of Mordecai and Esther?

4 If Esther and Mordecai believed in God why do you think, apart from the fasting in this chapter, there is no mention of God or other religious practices recorded in this book?

5 Despite their belief in God's sovereignty, Mordecai and Esther did not assume God would miraculously intervene: they took action. Why?

HOW DOES THIS

APPLY TO ME

6 How do we know when it is right to expect God to work supernaturally and when it's right to take the initiative?

7 What would you say to anyone who claims that because God does not appear to be working in a certain situation nor exerting his control, he must have abandoned them?

HOW DOES THIS | APPLY TO ME

8 'Work as if it all depended on you, pray as if it all depended on God.' In what area of your life do you need to take this advice onboard? If it's appropriate, share your thoughts in twos and then pray for each other.

WORSHIP

You may want to respond in a variety of ways after this session:

▶ Some may recognise they haven't given God control of a certain aspect of their life
▶ Some may realise that God wants them to take action in their situation
▶ Some may realise in a fresh sense that God has placed them where they are 'for such a time as this'

Some may find it helpful to write down their responses, some may like to pray with someone, others may like to show their commitment in a practical way by fasting like Esther did.

As you conclude this session reflect on the example of Jesus − he submitted himself completely to God's control and only acted according to his father's will. He recognised the importance of his task and knew that he had come to earth 'for such a time as this' (Rom. 5:6, Gal. 4:4).

FOR NEXT WEEK

It is easy to get caught up in the busyness of life. But this week, set some time aside to evaluate why God has planted you in your work/home/church situation. Why has he given you the opportunities he has and how does he want you to use them? In the light of your answers think through how your priorities, values and attitudes need to change. If it is appropriate, share your thoughts with your prayer partner.

FOR FURTHER STUDY

If You Want To Walk On Water You Have To Get Out Of The Boat by John Ortberg is a must-read for those serious about accepting God's plans for them in 'such a time as this'.

ACTIVITY PAGE

There are times in the Christian life for feasting and celebration but there are also times for fasting. Like Esther, we have a position of influence with the king, not with an earthly king but with the King of Kings. The apostle Peter calls us 'a chosen people, a royal priesthood, a holy nation, a people belonging to God' (1 Pet. 2:9). So we can use our royal position to bring people and situations before God.

Think about having a day of prayer and fasting in your church or in your home group. If you've never fasted before, start by just missing one meal and use the time to pray instead.

Below are a few practical suggestions that might be of help:

▶ Do some research as to why people in the Bible fasted (1 Sam. 7:6, Ezra 8:21, Joel 2:12–17).

▶ What are God's instructions about fasting? See Isaiah 58:1–14, Matthew 6:16–18.

▶ Discuss together the principles behind fasting – it does not give us increased leverage to get what we want from God but it sharpens our focus on him; it helps us recognise our dependence on him and is a means of submitting our will to his.

▶ Talk about how the fast will work practically – how long will you fast? What will you fast from? Do you have any medical concerns? What will you do if you feel really weak? Have you got a support network in place?

▶ Have someone or something specific to fast and pray for. It could be a world situation, an issue in your church or an individual's concern.

▶ Plan to celebrate the end of the fast by getting together. Set aside time to pray together, perhaps have a meal together but don't overeat or you'll feel really ill!

Some resources:

100 Days by Glenn Myers contains extracts from Operation World to give you pointers for prayer.

Prayer: Key to Revival by Paul Y. Cho is a book by the pastor of the world's largest church. He writes about prayer in general but also deals specifically with the link between prayer and fasting and whether fasting increases the effectiveness of prayer.

Other books on fasting include *Fasting* by Derek Prince and *The Hidden Power of Prayer and Fasting* by Mahesh Chavda.

A MATTER OF HONOUR

Aim: To give God back the place of honour in our lives

DIY programmes and garden makeovers have become hugely popular TV viewing because we're all interested in 'keeping up with the Jones'.' We can't help comparing ourselves to others and what we've got with what they've got. If we're honest, how we feel about ourselves, and our reputation, usually depends on being able to compare ourselves favourably with someone else. But God has a different criterion for measuring our value. Paradoxically, he says the way we find true honour and reputation is by giving him first place in our lives.

> *When Haman entered, the king asked him, 'What should be done for the man the king delights to honour?'*
>
> *Now Haman thought to himself, 'Who is there that the king would rather honour than me? So he answered the king, 'For the man the king delights to honour, have them bring a royal robe the king has worn and a horse the king has ridden, one with a royal crest placed on its head. Then let the robe and horse be entrusted to one of the king's most noble princes. Let them robe the man the king delights to honour, and lead him on the horse through the city streets, proclaiming before him, "This is what is done for the man the king delights to honour!"'*
>
> *'Go at once,' the king commanded Haman. 'Get the robe and the horse and do just as you have suggested for Mordecai the Jew, who sits at the king's gate. Do not neglect anything you have recommended.'*
>
> *So Haman got the robe and the horse. He robed Mordecai, and led him on horseback through the city streets, proclaiming before him, 'This is what is done for the man the king delights to honour!'*
>
> **Esther 6:6–11**

TO SET THE SCENE

Whom do we honour in society? In the Christian world whom do we honour? Why do we honour these people? What do our choices reveal about the values that are important to us? Look through some national newspapers, secular and Christian magazines to give you more ideas as you brainstorm together.

READ ESTHER 5:1–6:14

1 What's the evidence that Haman was obsessed with hatred towards Mordecai?

2 Examine each of these factors and decide which one was most responsible for Haman's attitude towards Mordecai. Explain your answer.
- Mordecai was a Jew
- Mordecai would not treat him with the honour his position deserved
- Mordecai was related to Queen Esther

3 Look at the speech in 6:7–9 and rate on a scale of 1–10 (1 being a little and 10 being a lot) how important each of these values were to Haman?
- Wealth
- Power
- Honour/recognition

4 To what extent do you see yourself in Haman?
- You have many blessings but let the one thing you don't have rob you of joy
- You care far too much about what other people think of you

5 What are the telltale signs that we're getting too caught up in pursuing our own honour?

6 In what ways can you see God working behind the scenes in chapter 6 to humble Haman and honour Mordecai?

WHAT DOES SEARCH THE BIBLE SAY? **7** Think of your favourite Bible characters: in what ways did God honour them?

8 What are the safeguards/risks when we let God look after our reputation and honour?

APPLY THIS TO MY CHURCH **9** As a church, what steps can you take to make sure we're honouring God?

WORSHIP

When we're preoccupied with our own reputation and honour, we don't give God the honour he deserves. We put ourselves, rather than him, in control of our lives. Sit around in a circle and in the middle of the room put an empty chair. The chair will have pieces of paper sellotaped all over it. Imagine that this chair is the throne in your life. Who or what do you need to get off the throne so that God can take his rightful place? Spend some time in quiet prayer, then get a piece of paper off the chair and write down who or what is coming off the throne. As you look at the empty chair, imagine God taking the place of honour and control in your life. End this session by singing or listening to songs that focus on God being our Lord and King.

FOR NEXT WEEK

Who in your church works hard behind the scenes but rarely gets publicly thanked or recognised? Perhaps it's the people on the coffee rota, those on the music team, or your child's Sunday school teacher. Write them a letter of thanks, send them some flowers, or do something to show that you recognise the work they do and honour them for it.

ACTIVITY PAGE

We all want to protect our reputation and honour. The desire to be loved and appreciated by others is a strong one!

'Living for an audience of One', living to please God rather than others and to promote his honour rather than our own, is a life long lesson.

Imagine the following scenarios. How would you advise these individuals to respond if they wanted to let God look after their reputation and honour? What are the possible consequences of the choices they make?

- ▶ Something you said has been taken out of context and reported to someone else in church. They now have a wrong impression of you and are making false assumptions about your views and opinions.

- ▶ Your husband is on the church leadership team. All the other leaders' wives take a prominent role in church life. You are involved in the children's work because there is a gap to fill rather than because it's your spiritual gift. You'd like to give up but are worried what other people might think.

- ▶ Your friends and family are expecting you to get promoted at your next review session. You'd like the promotion because it would mean added kudos and better financial security for your family. However, it would mean travelling away from home a lot and exposing yourself to temptations you know you're susceptible to.

Some verses to meditate on:

Isaiah 66:2 *'This is the one I esteem: he who is humble and contrite in spirit, and trembles at my word.'*

Psalm 84:11 *'For the Lord God is a sun and shield; the Lord bestows favour and honour; no good thing does he withhold from those whose walk is blameless.'*

John 12:26 *'Whoever serves me must follow me; and where I am, my servant will also be. My Father will honour the one who serves me.'*

THE BEST IS STILL TO COME

AIM

Aim: Learning to trust in God's timing

Some people like to give the impression that they're spiritual giants with a hot line to God. But actually we're all the same; dealing with the suffering and hurt that's part of being human, struggling to believe in our hearts what we know in our heads: that 'In all things God works together for the good of those who love him.' We've tried to find shortcuts to victorious Christian living but perhaps the secret is to take the long view – whatever good or bad happens in this life, in the light of eternity it is certainly true that 'the best is still to come.'

The king's edict granted the Jews in every city the right to assemble and protect themselves; to destroy, kill and annihilate any armed force of any nationality or province that might attack them and their women and children; and to plunder the property of their enemies. The day appointed for the Jews to do this in all the provinces of King Xerxes was the thirteenth day of the twelfth month, the month of Adar. A copy of the text of the edict was to be issued as law in every province and made known to the people of every nationality so that the Jews would be ready on that day to avenge themselves on their enemies.

The couriers, riding the royal horses, raced out, spurred on by the king's command. And the edict was also issued in the citadel of Susa.

Mordecai left the king's presence wearing royal garments of blue and white, a large crown of gold and a purple robe of fine linen. And the city of Susa held a joyous celebration. For the Jews it was a time of happiness and joy, gladness and honour. In every province and every city, wherever the edict of the king went, there was joy and gladness among the Jews, with feasting and celebrating. And many people of other nationalities became Jews because fear of the Jews had seized them.

Esther 8:11–17

TO SET THE SCENE

What has been the happiest day of your life? Think back to some special occasion or time in life and explain to the group why it was particularly memorable for you.

READ ESTHER 7:1-8:17

1 When the television soaps have a major cliff-hanger they record a couple of different endings to keep everyone guessing. How else could the story of Esther turned out? Think of the ways the main characters could have reacted differently.

WHAT DOES THE BIBLE SAY? **2** Why could the king not just revoke his edict? Why did he have to issue a new one? See Esther 8:8, Daniel 6:15.

3 The Jews started celebrating even before their victory. Why do you think they were so certain of success?

4 Explain how events had worked out for Mordecai far better than he could have imagined.

5 In the success of Mordecai and of the Jews as a whole, timing was crucial. Explain what difference good timing made in the following scenes:
- Esther's banquets 5:1-8, 7:1-6
- Haman's plea to Esther 7:6-10
- Getting the second edict to the Jews 8:10,13-14

6 Brainstorm all the thoughts that come to mind when you hear the phrase 'God's timing'.

WHAT DOES **7** God's timing meant Esther had to wait
– wait three days and hold two banquets
before she presented her request to the
THE BIBLE SAY? king. What does it mean to 'wait on God'?
Look at:

> ▶ Psalm 130
> ▶ Thessalonians 1:1–10
> ▶ Titus 2:11–15

8 Share together examples of occasions where
you have waited on God's timing and circumstances
have turned out better than you could have hoped or
planned for.

HOW DOES THIS **9** As Christians, how can we keep focused
on the truth that whatever happens in life
'the best is still to come'?
APPLY TO ME

WORSHIP

Each member of the group will be experiencing life in different ways. Give people time to commit their individual circumstances to God – to thank him for events that have turned out well and to bring before him issues that still need his touch. Then collectively affirm together the truth that 'the best is still to come!' Read Revelation 7:15–17, reflect on the wrongs which will be righted when we get to heaven and the royal status we'll fully enjoy. Like Mordecai, one day we will wear a crown (Rev 2:10) and be clothed in fine linen (Rev 19:8).

FOR NEXT WEEK

Using your answers to question 9, find a practical way to encourage someone who is going through difficult times that 'the best is still to come'.

FOR FURTHER STUDY

God Isn't In A Hurry by Warren Wiersbe reminds us of the lessons God wants to teach us in his waiting room.

When Heaven Is Silent by Ronald Dunn is helpful for people who have been waiting for God to intervene in their situation for a long time and are growing discouraged.

GREAT CELEBRATIONS

AIM

Aim: To celebrate our salvation

Larry Norman once sang 'Why should the devil have all the good music?' The secular world, as the book of Esther shows, knows how to party and celebrate – rarely are Christians accused of this. We're more likely to be labelled the 'frozen chosen'! We forget that celebrating was part of God's plan from the beginning. The Jews often had holidays and feasts to celebrate deliverance from their enemies and God's protection over them. And because of Jesus we too have so much to celebrate.

Mordecai recorded these events, and sent letters to all the Jews throughout the provinces of King Xerxes, near and far, to have them celebrate annually the fourteenth and fifteenth days of the month of Adar as the time when the Jews got relief from their enemies, and as the month when their sorrow was turned into joy and their mourning into a day of celebration. He wrote them to observe the days as feasting and joy and giving presents of food to one another and gifts to the poor.

So the Jews agreed to continue the celebration they had begun, doing what Mordecai had written to them. For Haman son of Hammedatha, the Agagite, enemy of all the Jews, had plotted against the Jews to destroy them and had cast the pur (that is, lot) for their ruin and destruction. But when the plot came to the king's attention, he issued written orders that the evil scheme Haman had devised against the Jews should come back onto his own head, and that he and his sons should be hanged on the gallows. (Therefore these days were called Purim, from the word pur.) Because of everything written in this letter and because of what they had seen and what had happened to them, the Jews took it upon themselves to establish the custom that they and their descendants and all who join them should without fail observe these two days every year, in the way prescribed and at the time appointed.

Esther 9:20–27

TO SET THE SCENE

If possible, meet earlier than usual and eat a meal or dessert together. Have a time of 'joy and feasting', relax and catch up with what's going on in each other's lives.

READ ESTHER 9:1–10:3

1 Esther 9:1: 'But now the tables were turned.' Look back over the whole story – how had the tables been turned for individuals and for events?

2 How would you describe the success of the Jews against their enemies?

WHAT DOES SEARCH THE BIBLE SAY?

3 The Jews were not always successful in defeating their enemies – just think back to the exile! Why were they victorious on this occasion? Why is it relevant that they didn't take any plunder (Esth. 9:10,15,16)? Look back at 1 Samuel 15:17–19.

4 What exactly were the Jews celebrating at Purim? Look at Esther 9:16,22.

WHAT DOES SEARCH THE BIBLE SAY?

5 What other occasions did the Jews celebrate and why? For some examples *(Unleavened bread)* look at:
  ▶ Exodus 12:1–14 *Passover – Deliverance*
  ▶ Leviticus 23:9–14 *Thank offering –*
  ▶ Leviticus 23:26–32 *Day of Atonement*
  ▶ Leviticus 23:33–36,39–43 *Feast Booths – Harvest.*

APPLY THIS TO
MY CHURCH

6 What does your church celebrate? Does it celebrate the same things as the Jews?

7 What can we learn from how the Jews celebrated at Purim?

HOW DOES THIS
APPLY TO ME

8 Mordecai wrote a record of events to remind the Jews how and why to celebrate. What helps you remember to celebrate your salvation?

HOW DOES THIS
APPLY TO ME

9 Purim was to be celebrated by successive generations.

▶ What do you want the next generation of Christians to be celebrating?

▶ What are the best ways we can pass on this Christian heritage?

WORSHIP

Jesus instructed us to celebrate our salvation often so that we wouldn't forget how and why he died (1 Cor. 11:23–26). As this is the last session it would be good to share communion together, celebrating all the Jesus did for us on the cross, remembering our personal deliverance from the enemy and thanking God for continuing to save people throughout history.

FOR FURTHER STUDY

John Ortberg's book *The Life You've Always Wanted* has a helpful chapter on 'The Practice of Celebration' that outlines some practical ideas of how to start celebrating.

FOR FUTURE WEEKS

Celebrating is a spiritual discipline we often neglect! Plan a celebration with your friends and family soon. Celebrate a traditional Christian festival, the anniversary of when you became a Christian, or a particular way that God has blessed you recently. Enjoy a meal, give small gifts to one another and incorporate others into your celebrations by showing a special act of kindness to them.

ACTIVITY PAGE

Reread the book of Esther and reflect on what God has been teaching you. Perhaps share your thoughts with a prayer partner or friend. Like Mordecai, keep a record, noting down in a spiritual journal what you have learnt in these past few weeks and the commitments you've made in response. Make a date in your diary to come back and celebrate these truths and commitments.

Some questions to help you get started:

▶ What have you learnt about God and the way he acts?

▶ What encouragements/challenges have you had from the book?

▶ Is God calling you to a special task as he did Esther and Mordecai?

▶ Is God calling you to be more devoted in your prayer life?

▶ Can you see God working in quiet ways in your life?

▶ Is there a particular area of your life where you have to trust God more?

▶ Is there a particular area of your life where you need to acknowledge God's control?

▶ Like Haman, do you have some hatred and bitterness from your past that you have to deal with?

LEADERS' GUIDE

TO HELP YOU LEAD

You may have led a housegroup many times before or this may be your first time. Here is some advice on how to lead these studies:

▶ As a group leader, you don't have to be an expert or a lecturer. You are there to facilitate the learning of the group members – helping them to discover for themselves the wisdom in God's word. You should not be doing most of the talking or dishing out the answers, whatever the group expects from you!

▶ You do need to be aware of the group's dynamics, however. People can be quite quick to label themselves and each other in a group situation. One person might be seen as the expert, another the moaner who always has something to complain about. One person may be labelled as quiet and not be expected to contribute; another person may always jump in with something to say. Be aware of the different type of individuals in the group, but don't allow the labels to stick. You may need to encourage those who find it hard to get a word in, and quieten down those who always have something to say. Talk to members between sessions to find out how they feel about the group.

▶ The sessions are planned to try and engage every member in active learning. Of course you cannot force anyone to take part if they don't want to, but it won't be too easy to be a spectator. Activities that ask everyone to write down a word or talk in twos, and then report back to the group, are there for a reason. They give everyone space to think and form their opinions, even if not everyone voices them out loud.

▶ Do adapt the sessions for your group as you feel is appropriate. Some groups may know each other very well and will be prepared to talk at a deep level. New groups may take a bit of time to get to know each other before making themselves vulnerable, but encourage members to share their lives with each other.

▶ You probably won't be able to tackle all the questions in each session so decide in advance which ones are most appropriate to your group and situation.

▶ Encourage a number of replies to each question. The study is not about finding a single right answer, but about sharing experiences and thoughts in order to find out how to apply the Bible to people's lives. When brainstorming, don't be too quick to evaluate the contributions. Write everything down and then have a look to see which suggestions are worth keeping.

▶ Similarly, encourage everyone to ask questions, voice doubts and discuss difficulties. Some parts of the Bible are difficult to understand. Sometimes the Christian faith throws up paradoxes. Painful things happen to us that make it difficult to see what God is doing. A housegroup should be a safe place to express all of this. If discussion doesn't resolve the issue, send everyone away to pray about it between sessions, and ask your minister for advice.

▶ Give yourself time in the week to read through the Bible passage and the questions. Read the Leaders' notes for the session, as different ways of presenting the questions are sometimes suggested. However during the session don't be too quick to come in with the answer – sometimes people need space to think.

▶ Delegate as much as you like! The easiest activities to delegate are reading the text, and the worship sessions, but there are other ways to involve the group members. Giving people responsibility can help them own the session much more.

▶ Pray for group members by name, that God would meet with them during the week. Pray for the group session, for a constructive and helpful time. Ask the Lord to equip you as you lead the group.

THE STRUCTURE OF EACH SESSION

Feedback: find out what people remember from the previous session, or if they have been able to act during the week on what was discussed last time.

To set the scene: an activity or a question to get everyone thinking about the subject to be studied.

Bible reading: it's important actually to read the passage you are studying during the session. Ask someone to prepare this in advance or go around the group reading a verse or two each. Don't assume everyone will be happy to read out loud.

Questions and activities: adapt these as appropriate to your group. Some groups may enjoy a more activity-based approach; some may prefer just to discuss the questions. Try out some new things!

Worship: suggestions for creative worship and prayer are included, which give everyone an opportunity to respond to God, largely individually. Use these alongside singing or other group expressions of worship. Add a prayer time with opportunities to pray for group members and their families and friends.

For next week: this gives a specific task to do during the week, helping people to continue to think about or apply what they have learned.

Further study: suggestions are given for those people who want to study the themes further. These could be included in the housegroup if you feel it's appropriate and if there is time.

WHAT YOU NEED

A list of materials that are needed is printed at the start of each session in the Leaders' Guide. In addition you will probably need:

Bibles: the main Bible passage is printed in the book so that all the members can work from the same version. It is useful to have other Bibles available, or to ask everyone to bring their own, so that other passages can be referred to.

Paper and pens: for people who need more space than is in the book!

Flip chart: it is helpful to write down people's comments during a brainstorming session, so that none of the suggestions is lost. They may not be space for a proper flip chart in the average lounge, and having one may make it feel too much like a business meeting or lecture. Try getting someone to write on a big sheet of paper on the floor or coffee table, and then stick this up on the wall with blu-tack.

GROUND RULES

How do people know what is expected of them in a housegroup situation? Is it ever discussed, or do we just pick up clues from each other? You may find it helpful to discuss some ground rules for the housegroup at the start of this course, even if your group has been going a long time. This also gives you an opportunity to talk about how you, as the leader, see the group. Ask everyone to think about what they want to get out of the course. How do they want the group to work? What values do they want to be part of the group's experience; honesty, respect, confidentiality? How do they want their contributions to be treated? You could ask everyone to write down three ground rules on slips of paper and put them in a bowl. Pass the bowl around the group. Each person takes out a rule and reads it, and someone collates the list. Discuss the ground rules that have been suggested and come up with a top five. This method enables everyone to contribute fairly anonymously. Alternatively, if your group are all quite vocal, have a straight discussion about it!

NB Not all questions in each session are covered, some are self-explanatory.

ICONS

 The aim of the session

 Engaging with the world

 Investigate what else the Bible says

 How does this apply to me?

 What about my church?

SESSION 1

TO SET THE SCENE

If this is the first time your group has met, introduce yourselves and spend some time getting to know each other. This first exercise is designed as a fun way to think through your motives and how you operate in secular situations. Hopefully, other peoples' comments will challenge your thinking about how you respond to 'gospel opportunities' in the secular world.

N.B. As you examine this secular world, some group members may be concerned about Esther's morals. She slept with a pagan king and then became one of his many wives! Don't get too side-tracked by this discussion. We need to recognise that this is one of the places in the Bible where the author is describing a situation for us rather than prescribing it as something we need to follow.

1 The court/palace was influential because the king was militarily and politically powerful; he had a vast empire, and support from all the key statesmen. It was a place of great opulence because it was here that the king's tremendous success and power were displayed. There were beautiful gardens, couches and jewelled pavements! The palace was a place of tremendous generosity – the guest list was long and the wine flowed freely. It was a male-dominated world where men had the ear of the king and decisions were based on his whim.

2 His riches – the excessive banquet, the gardens, and individual wine glasses. Generosity – his guest list included all the people in the citadel of Susa and the wine was on tap. Used to getting his own way – no one curbed the excesses of the revelry, he was affronted when Vashti did not appear. Easily influenced – he was influenced by the wine and listened without question to the advice of his wise men, even being willing to depose his queen.

3 Xerxes was influenced by the desire to be admired and respected, to appear strong and in control, to enjoy women and revelry, and to get his own way.

4 One might be concerned for Esther's safety, given that Vashti was clearly dispensable; she was not allowed to explain herself or have a second chance. The treatment of Vashti was symptomatic of how women in general were viewed – as property, to obey and please men, with no rights of their own. This picture of court life prepares us to recognise the danger Esther faced when she confronts the king about the plight of the Jews.

5 That God used such secular people, places and events reminds us that he works in unexpected ways. God is interested in all the parts of our life and no situation is too desperate for him to work in. It reminds us our evangelism must reach these secular situations: we cannot just expect people to come to church if they want to be converted.

6 We separate God from our secular life for many reasons – we think he may not feel 'at home'; we believe that if we integrated him into our work situation then he might want to change the way we behave, we'd have to take time and pray about situations, we'd have to talk to others about God etc; perhaps we feel that God might limit our freedom if we allowed him into every area of our lives; sometimes we believe that God is only interested in our productivity if we're serving him in ministry.

7 Work life – we can pray about our work situations, colleagues and major decisions throughout the day. We can bring a Christian perspective to all our interactions, from business discussions to casual chats. Family life – we can make time for family prayers and devotionals, make important Christian events such as Easter part of our traditional family celebrations, and talk about God and the Bible naturally. Social life – when we're relaxing with Christian friends, we can encourage one another in our spiritual lives and talk about God together, we can be involved in church social activities, and we can see our times with non-Christian friends as opportunities to represent Christ.

8 We can share the gospel explicitly but we can also bring God's point of view into the workplace by the values and priorities that we advocate, our treatment of other colleagues, our integrity and dedication, our respect for the boss, our lack of gossip and manipulation tactics, and our willingness to do what is good rather than always being governed by personal rights.

9 To be an effective gospel witness in secular situations, we need to protect our own devotional life and maintain close links with our church. It would be good to have a prayer partner or someone to whom we can be accountable. We can take practical measures to preserve our testimony – not being alone with a member of the opposite sex in a potentially compromising situation, for example.

SESSION 2

MATERIALS NEEDED

Candles and matches

CDs, tapes and a music system if you'd like to use it in the worship section

TO SET THE SCENE

Thinking about the different Christian taboos and how they have changed may help the group decide which aspects of Christian behaviour are cultural and traditional and which aspects reflect key values you want to preserve.

1 We learn the extent of Xerxes' appetite for beautiful women and that there were no limits in his pursuit of pleasure – the whole realm was searched for virgins for his harem. The lavishness of their beauty regime reveals again the extent of his wealth and resources. His every whim and selfish tendency were satisfied regardless of how this affected others – some girls may have lived as concubines, isolated from their families, never being recalled by the king. The banquets, holiday and gifts show his generosity.

2 Mordecai was related to King Saul, the first Israelite king.

3 Esther was not rude and overbearing: instead, her pleasant disposition won her favour in the eyes of Hegei and everyone else she met, including the king (2:15, 17). She listened to Hegei's advice as to what to take with her to the king. She was more than compliant in the situation, she was positive and eager to please.

4 Although Esther did not indulge in some of the extravagance suggested, she did eat the king's food and use the beauty treatments. This contrasts with Daniel and his friends who only ate vegetables and water, presumably because the king's food had been sacrificed to idols and was not kosher. Daniel had a pleasant disposition, as did Esther, but they made different choices as to how many non-Jewish practices they would accommodate.

5 We don't know why Esther concealed her Jewish identity except that Mordecai told her to. Perhaps he feared she'd encounter the bitterness of men like Haman. The fact that she doesn't disclose who she really is prepares us for the trouble she will face later on in the story. The author doesn't despise her for her secrecy – clearly this isn't the main point of the account. Esther's example shows

that, at times, it may be prudent to conceal our faith but for the most part we need to listen to Jesus' command to let our faith make a difference where we are. Secrecy is the exception rather than the rule.

6   Missionaries working where Christianity is forbidden usually find evangelism most effective when it is done in a low-key manner. Perhaps, at times, broadcasting our Christianity at work doesn't help our cause. Instead, we should concentrate on working with integrity and thus earn a platform to share our faith.

7   Esther and Mordecai were both loyal to the regime and to the king. They were courteous and had dispositions that won them favour. However, they maintained their loyalty to God, to their fellow Jews and used their influential positions for good. We can share the loyalty of Esther and Mordecai in our work situations, working with integrity, respecting those in authority, listening to those with wise advice. But at the same time we can also stand for God's priorities in a non-offensive way, we can take action to protect and promote God's values and his people.

8   We should work hard in the secular world, seeking to gain people's favour where possible so that the only offence is the message of the cross. We need to take care to preserve the integrity of our testimony, not giving God a bad press because of our attitudes or behaviour. We should submit with respect to ruling authorities as far as we're able until their laws contravene God's laws. If we do need to break secular laws, we must be prepared to face the consequences.

SESSION 3

TO SET THE SCENE

We tend to think of our 'enemy' as a soldier in combat gear with guns blazing. But the term is much broader. Big business and organisational structures can be enemies of the poor, the popular drive for wealth and materialism can be an enemy of all age groups, our tolerant postmodern culture can be an enemy of Christianity and so is the Devil etc. Today our enemies are often hard to spot because their influence is subtle. As you talk about people's enemies help them examine their own values, see the impact of their own bitterness and re-evaluate which issues are worth taking a stand on.

1   The author contrasts the behaviour and fortune of the two characters throughout the story. He starts by highlighting the fact that Mordecai's good deeds go unrewarded by the king but Haman gets rewarded for no reason. In 3: 1 we expect the king will reward Mordecai for uncovering the assassination plot but surprisingly it is Haman he remembers. We also see a contrast in values and principles, as Mordecai will not bow down to Haman despite the king's orders.

2   Exodus 17 explains that the Amalekites were the first group of people to attack the Israelites after they had escaped from Egypt. Subsequently God and his people would always be at war with this nation. In 1 Samuel 15 king Saul defeats the Amalekites and the prophet Samuel puts their king Agag to death. Mordecai and Haman are successors of this long-standing dispute.

3   Haman accused the Jews of having different customs to the rest of the empire and of ignoring the king's laws. He encouraged the king to believe that the Jews were a menace to his rule because they were so subversive. He also made it seem as though he was personally protecting the king by offering to finance the extermination himself. In all his conversations with the king, Haman was careful not to mention that the group he was targeting was the Jews.

4   In the NIV the word 'each' is repeated in v12 to underline that each of the people groups in each of the provinces etc were told of the edict. The various messengers are also emphasised. In v13 the word 'all' is repeated and the innocent people like women and children are highlighted. In v14 the word 'every' is repeated – all Jews understood what was going to happen to them, no one was left in ignorance.

5   The edict would be carried out in eleven months' time. This time delay was agony for the Jews. They knew they were about to be executed but there was nowhere

to escape to since the Persian Empire covered the known world! In the meantime anti-Jewish feeling could be whipped up by Haman's men and ordinary people encouraged to get ready to plunder and kill the Jews. But the time delay also gave Esther an opportunity to present her case to the king and win him over.

6 From this account we are reminded how we too try to excuse personal hatred and bitterness, we try and make it sound legitimate and even right. Like Haman, we often oppose those who are different to ourselves, we allow hatred to pass and intensify from one generation to the next, we try and get others to see the situation from our perspective and to see us in a good light. However we try and conceal it, hatred and bitterness consume us and spread to others. Hatred is dangerous and has tremendous power to hurt others.

7 Racism may be more of an issue in some churches and communities than others. Encourage the group to see their own prejudices and what the possible outcomes could be.

8 We can come to God and ask his forgiveness for our bitterness, we can pray that God would help us recognise the person's humanity and love them as he does. If we've been hurt by someone we can pray for them, do good to them and say good about them. Sometimes it may be appropriate to discuss the issue along the lines of Matthew 18:15–17. In all cases it is worth remembering our own faults and failings rather than dwelling on the faults of others and the hurt they have caused us (Mt. 7:3–5).

9 God's enemies are not a particular nation or class of people; they are those who refuse his offer of salvation, refuse to live life with him at the centre, refuse to acknowledge their sin (Phil. 3:18–19). We all were enemies of God at one time (Rom. 5:9–11). Becoming a Christian has made us friends of God (Jas. 2:23) – we are now reconciled to him (Rom. 5:1). But at times we're still disobedient to his will, we ignore him and act like his enemies rather than his friends. We don't live like his children (Rom. 5:11–14) and this strains, though does not break, our friendship with him.

10 A friendship with God, like any friendship, needs to be cultivated. We need to spend time with him, reading his word, meditating on it and praying. It helps to confess our sins daily and keep short accounts with God. It is also beneficial to surround ourselves with those who spur us on spiritually. If we make every effort to maintain our relationship with God, it is more difficult to act like his enemy and ignore and disobey him.

SESSION 4

MATERIALS NEEDED:

Pens and paper for the worship session

TO SET THE SCENE

Use these questions to encourage your group to start thinking about the issue of 'control', the particular areas they struggle with and why. Use the last question to introduce the main issue of the session – the tension between human responsibility and divine sovereignty.

N.B. God's name isn't mentioned in the book and yet at every turn we see him working behind the scenes. Use this session to encourage the group that even if they can't see God in their own situation or in the lives of unbelieving family members, he is still present and at work. God wants us to learn to trust him in faith and it is often only with hindsight that we'll see how he was acting on our behalf.

1   If all the Jews were wiped out, then God's promise to Abraham would be nullified. God's promise about a Jewish Messiah to save the world would be impossible – the whole plan of salvation history would have been knocked off course.

2   Esther was reluctant to go and see the king because she faced death if she entered his presence without a summons. More than that, though, she felt her pleadings with the king would do little good – it had been thirty days since she'd been invited to go and see him. She felt she wasn't in favour at that moment.

3   Mordecai was a strong and pro-active character. He believed in God's sovereignty, that God would keep his promise to Abraham to protect and prosper the Jews. He also believed in human responsibility – that God had a plan in bringing Esther to the palace so she needed to be obedient to it. Esther too believed in God's sovereignty – 'If I perish, I perish' but at the same time she believed that it made a difference to God what humans did. So she suggested a severe three day twenty-four hour fast. Her actions in going to the king showed she was a very brave woman.

4   The fact that there is no mention of God and few references to religious practices in the book actually highlights God's involvement in the story. We can detect God in every coincidence – Mordecai just happened to overhear the plot to assassinate Xerxes, for example. The fact that God's involvement is not overt is very true to life – often we believe in our hearts that God is at work but there is little evidence of it at the present time, we can only see his hand in hindsight. Because God didn't intervene dramatically the need for human action is emphasised.

5   After Mordecai's speech it is clear that both he and Esther believed that God had placed her in the palace for a special reason – to save the Jews. They did pray and fast for God to work but at the same time they acknowledged God's hand in events by giving Esther this unique position.

6   It is often very difficult to know what to do in any given situation. But Esther's plan of praying and fasting and at the same time taking what logical steps she could is often a good place to start. If we keep submitting our will to God's and praying for his guidance we can be sure that if we take the wrong step he will put a stop to it. And even if God's hand is not obvious we know that he is at work behind the scenes so our role is to keep on being faithful, whatever that might look like in our situation.

7   It is easy to conclude that if a situation doesn't turn out as we think it should, God lacks control and has abandoned us. We need to remember that we only see part of the picture and God sees the whole. He is often working in ways we can't see or anticipate – no one would have dreamed that the numbers of Christians in China would have risen so dramatically under a strict communist regime, for example. We need to take care not to expect God to act as we would and to appreciate his ways are bigger than ours. He did not promise us a life of ease but called us to live for him by faith rather than by sight (2 Cor. 5:7). Knowing all that Jesus did for us on the cross and looking back over God's hand in all the events recorded in the Bible, we should take heart that God will never abandon us and rather is working on our behalf (Rom. 8:37–39).

SESSION 5

MATERIALS NEEDED

Flip chart or large sheet of paper and pens, newspapers, secular and Christian magazines for 'To set the scene' exercise.

A chair with blank pieces of paper sellotaped all over it

Instruments or tapes/CDs and music system if required for the worship section

TO SET THE SCENE

We can tell what character qualities and values are important to our society and to us by looking at the people we honour. We usually make heroes out of the people we'd most like to resemble. Your group can discuss whether as Christians our value system is all that much different from the secular world – do we honour Christians who are successful in secular terms or do we honour those who have godly characters or do the two categories overlap?

1   Haman had so much to be pleased about – he was in great favour with the king and queen, he was invited to their private banquet, he'd been given a position of much influence in the royal court, he had a lot of wealth, and he had friends and family. And yet he couldn't enjoy any of it because he hated the sight of Mordecai (5:13). Haman knew the Jews were going to be exterminated but he couldn't wait to get rid of Mordecai. He wasn't willing to kill Mordecai quietly, he wanted him publicly executed on a huge gallows. This is all evidence of an obsessive hatred of Mordecai.

2   Clearly the fact that Mordecai was a Jew was a problem for Haman. He mentions it in 3:6 and again in 5:13. However, as the Jews were soon going to be exterminated, it seems that Haman's main problem was the lack of respect/honour Mordecai showed him (5:9). As far as we can tell, Haman didn't know about Mordecai's royal connections, so this can't be used to explain his behaviour.

3   Wealth didn't seem to be of primary importance to Haman – he didn't ask for money or riches and seems to have enough already (5:11). Power was more important – Haman wanted to share in the king's status and power by wearing his robe and riding his horse. Honour seems the main motivation (in the NIV the word 'honour' is repeated seven times in chapter 6). He wanted to be promoted more than any of the other nobles, he wanted everyone to see and hear about his good fortune.

4 Encourage people to share as much as they are able. Concentrate the discussion particularly on the second part of the question. We often care more for what other people think about us, our public reputation and honour, than what God thinks about us. We tend to live to please others more than we live to please him.

5 When we're looking after our own honour and reputation, whether at work or church, we keep tasks and projects to ourselves, we take all the credit and don't want others to be involved in case they make a mistake. We're anxious to promote the good we do and to hide or excuse our failings. We care more about what others think of us and the impression we're creating, than about what we're doing.

6 God works behind the scenes in the apparent coincidences. For example, the king just happened to wake up and the record of Mordecai discovering the assassination plot just happened to be read to him. Also it so happened that Mordecai had not been rewarded for his loyalty to the king and Haman was the only one there when the king wanted advice.

7 People may mention a range of Bible characters. Encourage them to see that honour is given by God in his timing. For example, Joseph and Job went through much suffering before God honoured them in their lives with tangible things like wealth, power, and status. For others like Mary, the mother of Jesus, and the apostle Paul, there was not much honour in terms of public acclamation. Their honour is in the example and the legacy they pass on to believers.

8 When we let God look after our reputation we have the safety of knowing that it does not depend on the fickleness of other people's opinion of us; it does not depend on our performance and it is not something we need to strive to preserve. We have a sense of freedom that we are able to 'do the right thing' regardless of the consequences for us. However, there are risks – we may not receive the honour our contemporaries do, we may be misunderstood and unable to stand up for our rights.

9 As a church we honour God by making him the focal point of our services, by promoting his agenda rather than ours in the community, by striving to achieve high standards in our ministries, and by our care and compassion for others.

SESSION 6

MATERIALS NEEDED:

Flip chart or large sheets of paper and pens for the brainstorming question

TO SET THE SCENE

This icebreaker is not meant to put anyone under any pressure but to help you get to know each other better. If people can think of the happiest day of their life so far then encourage them to share it, if not don't worry. The point is that often we look back to happy memories with nostalgia and a tinge of regret as if life has never been the same since. Even as Christians we rarely believe or act as though the best is still to come.

1   The king could have had Esther killed for coming into his presence; he could have lost his patience with her for not voicing her request or been angry that she had not made her nationality known; she could have got tongue-tied and inadvertently implicated the king as well as Haman in the plot against the Jews and so faced his wrath; the king could have stuck by his decision to exterminate the Jews and to back his chief advisor.

2   It was law that the King of Persia's edicts could not be revoked, so Xerxes could only issue a second contradictory edict to save the Jewish people.

3   The Jews were confident of success because – an edict signed in the king's name and stamped with his seal gave them permission to defend themselves and made their enemies wary of opposing them; everyone got to know about the second edict which was law; the speed with which the edict was written and delivered by the king's couriers indicated royal approval; the Jews were able to prepare themselves for attack; Mordecai's prominence and the confidence of the Jews made people fear them.

4   Mordecai was given the king's signet ring, indicating he now had the power and status Haman once had; he was effectively the Prime Minister. Mordecai was also given Haman's estate, royal robes and a crown. He was even permitted to write what he wanted in the king's edict.

5 By being patient in the timing of the banquets, Esther aroused the king's interest and by persuading him to come to a second banquet he effectively agreed to her request without knowing what it was (5:8). The timing of the banquets also meant Haman built the gallows where he'd be hung and Mordecai was brought to the king's attention, ready to take over Haman's position. The timing was perfect in Esther's scene with Haman – just as the king walked in, Haman seemed to be mauling her. Because of the king's own involvement in the plot against the Jews, Haman's indiscretion was an excellent excuse for the king to get rid of him. Timing was also crucial in issuing the second edict – it meant the Jews had time to prepare to defend themselves and also made sure that their enemies knew they were not only opposing the Jews but effectively the king as well.

6 God's timing is often not the same as ours; it usually means waiting and trusting in God; it means God wants us to learn lessons along the way; it is often painful to wait; the way events unfold means that when the thing we've been waiting for happens, we know that it is only God who has done it; at times God moves faster than us and asks us to leave our comfort zones and trust him for a new thing.

7 Waiting on God is not a passive activity in which we do nothing. Waiting on God is an active trust in him and his word, where we're ready and equipped for action looking out for him like a watchman. As we wait for God, whether it is for him to act in our situation or for him to come again, we're to get on with holy living, resisting sin and temptation, serving and becoming more like him.

8 Encourage people to share, as they are able. Be sensitive to those who despite 'waiting on God' are still going through difficult times.

9 We need to find ways to get our eyes off the present and focus them on God and our eternal future. This is a daily decision we can help ourselves make as we meditate on Scripture, trust in God's promises, pray, meet with other Christians, and help others in need.

SESSION 7

ERIALS NEEDED:

Bread and wine if you are going to celebrate communion together

Plates, bowls, cutlery and food if you are going to eat a meal or dessert together

TO SET THE SCENE

Be like the Jews and celebrate a time of 'joy and feasting' together. Eating a meal or dessert as a group is a good way to relax, get to know each other better and just catch up with what's going on in people's lives. You will need to give people advance warning if you're meeting earlier than usual or if you'd like them to bring some food to share.

1   Haman, instead of being honoured by the king, was hung as punishment for plotting to exterminate the Jews. Esther started life as an ordinary Jewish girl but rose to prominence as queen of Persia. Mordecai was about to be hung for not honouring Haman but ended up inheriting Haman's estate and role as chief advisor to the king. Ironically,on the very day the Jews were to be exterminated they had a massive victory over their enemies.

2   The Jews were hugely successful. They were prepared to attack their enemies. In total they killed 800 men in the citadel of Susa and Haman's sons. In the provinces the Jews killed 75,000 men.

3   The Jews were victorious because they were ready to attack; because Mordecai's prominence won them the support of the nobles and officials; because fear ensured other nations were on their side and because they had two days rather than one to kill their enemies in Susa. God probably worked all these factors together to bring victory to the Jews because they had been obedient to him − they had fasted and prayed; they recognised his hand in events and celebrated the occasion as Purim when God delivered them rather than when they defeated their enemies; and they didn't take any plunder − five hundred years ago when the Jews disobeyed God and kept the Amalekites' (Haman's ancestors) goods, God took away Saul's crown.

4   The Jews were celebrating victory and rest after defeating their enemies, and joy after the threat of extinction was taken away. They were no longer going to die but had all of life to look forward to.

5 Exodus 12 – the Jews celebrated Passover remembering their deliverance from Egypt. Leviticus 23:9–14 – they celebrated the festival of First Fruits thanking God that he supplied all their physical needs. Leviticus 23:26–32 – they celebrated the Day of Atonement when God cleansed the people from their sins. Leviticus 23:33–36 – they celebrated the Feast of Tabernacles remembering the Israelites living in tents during their forty years in the desert.

6 We celebrate baptisms/dedications, confirmations, weddings, church anniversaries, funerals, communion, and harvest festivals. Like the Jews, we remember our deliverance from the enemy (sin) in our communion service and we acknowledge God's provision and blessings in our life on these other occasions. However, perhaps even in our celebration times we're slow to admit that everything we are and have comes from God and instead we feel proud of our own achievements.

7 At Purim, the Jews rested and feasted together and they gave gifts to the poor. We can learn from the Jewish example to have a greater sense of community in our times of celebration, to see our times with the church family as social times. We can also incorporate others into our celebrations – perhaps giving an impromptu financial gift to a missionary or Christian charity, giving a practical gift to a needy church member. N.B Some background information on Purim may be helpful here: It was the noisiest and most boisterous of all the Jewish festivals. Chanting, booing and cheering made the service look a bit like a pantomime and there was great rejoicing in the celebrations afterwards. This festival reminds us that God made people to celebrate. Celebrating God and all he has done – that is true worship. Purim shows us worship doesn't have to be staid and formal. It can be very exuberant and joyful.

8 Communion helps us remember our salvation. Sometimes reflecting on certain passages of Scripture, revisiting the place where we became Christians, writing in a spiritual journal, and certain visual objects also have this effect.

9 Your group may come up with many different ideas – certainly the main thing we want the next generation to be celebrating is their own faith in God. There are many ways that we can try and pass on this heritage – talking about spiritual things, making celebrations fun and interactive, praying for the next generation, reflecting a love for the Lord in our own lives.

WORSHIP

In some cases, it might be appropriate to mention to your minister about your wish to share communion together as a group. Adapt this section to your church setting.

FURTHER READING

The book of Esther brings up many issues that you might like to look at further.

Here is a list of books to help you get started:

100 Days – Glenn Myers

Prayer: key to revival – Paul Y. Cho

Prayer – O. Hallesby

Listening to God – Joyce Huggett

Discovering God's Will – Sinclair B. Ferguson

Fasting – Derek Prince

Hidden Power Of Prayer And Fasting – Mahesh Chavda.

God Isn't In A Hurry – Warren Wiersbe

When Heaven Is Silent – Ronald Dunn

Living Proof – Jim Petersen

Issues Facing Christians Today – John Stott

A Long Way East Of Eden – Peter Lowman

If You Want To Walk On Water You've Got To Get Out Of The Boat – John Ortberg

The Life You've Always Wanted – John Ortberg

For a more lighthearted look at the story of Esther, why not watch the Veggie Tales video *Esther: The Girl Who Became Queen*.

FURTHER INFORMATION

If you would like further information and resources the following organisations may be of help. They will be able to tell you what is going on in your locality and how you can get involved:

The Evangelical Alliance
186 Kennington Park Road
London
SE11 4BT
Tel 020 7207 2100
Email – info@eauk.org

Care for the Family
PO Box 488
Cardiff
CF15 7YY
Tel 02920 810800
Email – mail@cff.org.uk

Faithworks
Tel 0207 450 9050
www.faithworkscampaign.org

Open Doors
PO Box 6
Witney
Oxon
OX29 6WG
Tel 01993 885400
Email – helpdesk@opendoorsuk.org

Rebuild
16 Kingston Road
London
SW19 1JZ
Tel 020 82395581
Email – info@rebuild.org.uk

TEARFUND
100 Church Road
Teddington
TW11 8QE
Tel 020 8977 9144
www.tearfund.org

London Institute for Contemporary Christianity
Tel 0207 3999555
www.licc.org.uk